T0101544

CONTENTS

GENIE IN A BOTTLE

Words and Music by STEVE KIPNER,
DAVID FRANK and PAMELA SHEYNE

Medium beat

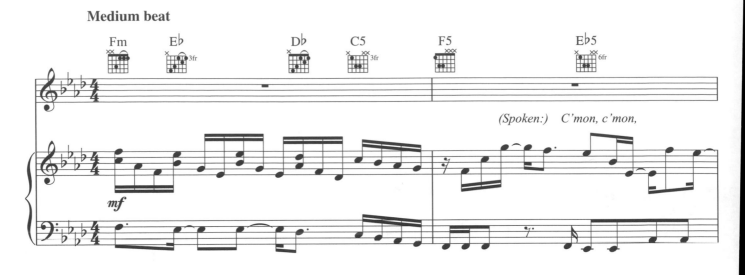

© 1998, 1999 EMI APRIL MUSIC INC., STEPHEN A. KIPNER MUSIC, GRIFF GRIFF MUSIC and APPLETREESONGS LTD.
All Rights for STEPHEN A. KIPNER MUSIC and GRIFF GRIFF MUSIC Controlled and Administered by EMI APRIL MUSIC INC.
All Rights for APPLETREESONGS LTD. Controlled and Administered by UNIVERSAL MUSIC - CAREERS
All Rights Reserved   International Copyright Secured   Used by Permission

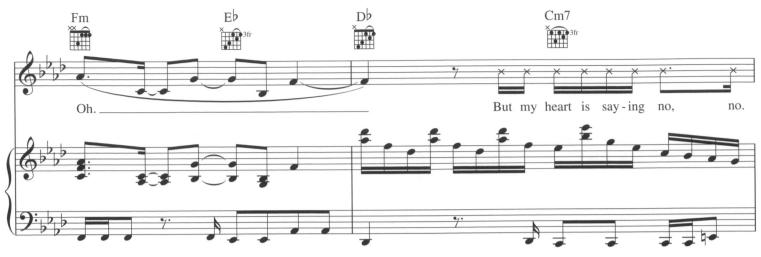

Oh. _____ But my heart is say-ing no, no.

If you wan-na be with me, ba-by, there's a price to pay. I'm a ge-nie in a bot-

-tle; you got-ta rub me the right way. If you wan-na be with

me, I can make your wish come true. You got-ta make a big ___ im - pres-

sion. Got-ta like what you do. _____ I'm a ge-nie in a bot-tle, ba-by.

You got-ta rub _ me the right way, hon - ey. _ I'm a ge-nie in a bot-tle, ba-by.

Come, _ come, come on and let me out.   true.   Just come and set _ me free, _

_____ ba - by, _ and I'll be with you. _____ I'm a ge-nie in a bot-tle, ba-by.

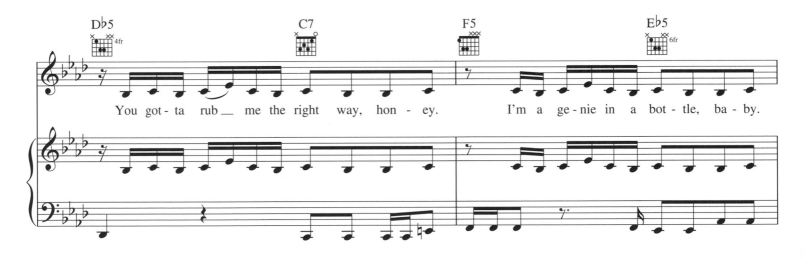

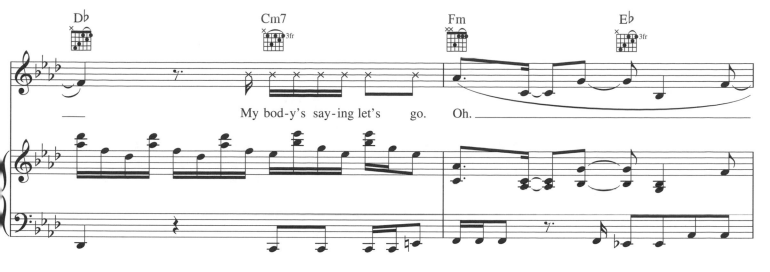

My bod-y's say-ing let's go. Oh. _____

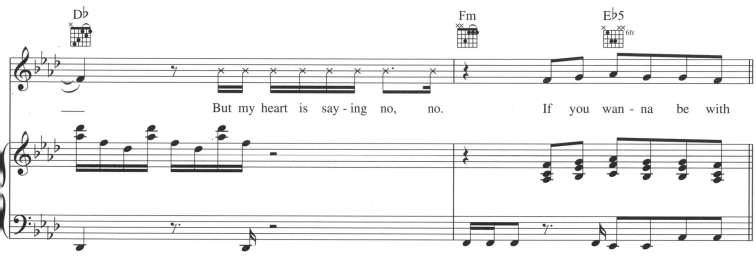

But my heart is say-ing no, no. If you wan-na be with

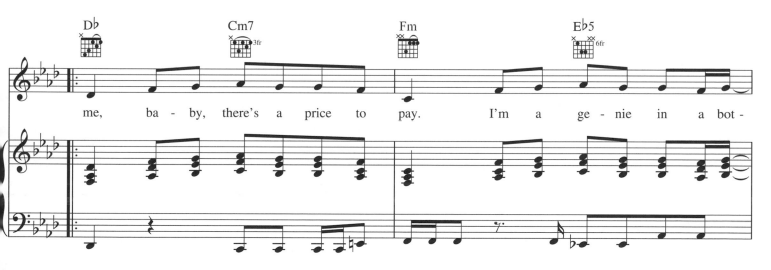

me, ba-by, there's a price to pay. I'm a ge-nie in a bot-

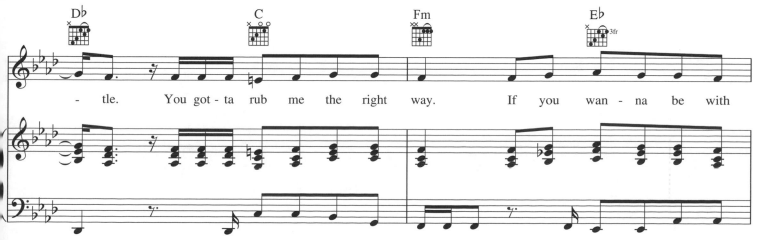

-tle. You got-ta rub me the right way. If you wan-na be with

WHAT A GIRL WANTS

Words and Music by SHELLY PEIKEN
and GUY ROCHE

Moderately fast

What a girl wants, what a girl needs, what a girl wants, what a girl needs, yeah __ come on. Ooh _____ ah yeah.

I wan-na thank you for giv-ing me time __ to breathe. __

© 1999 HIDDEN PUN MUSIC INC., SUSHI TOO, UNIVERSAL MUSIC - MGB SONGS and MANUITI L.A.
All Rights for HIDDEN PUN MUSIC INC. and SUSHI TOO Controlled and Administered by EMI BLACKWOOD MUSIC INC.
All Rights for MANUITI L.A. Controlled and Administered by UNIVERSAL MUSIC - MGB SONGS
All Rights Reserved   International Copyright Secured   Used by Permission

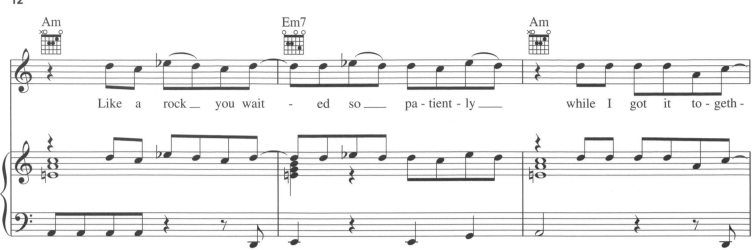

Like a rock __ you wait - ed so __ pa - tient - ly __ while I got it to - geth -

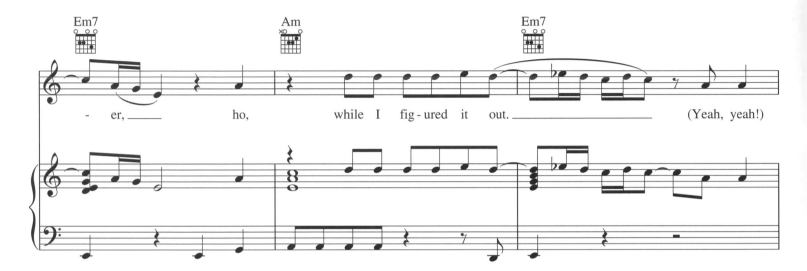

- er, ___ ho, while I fig - ured it out. _____ (Yeah, yeah!)

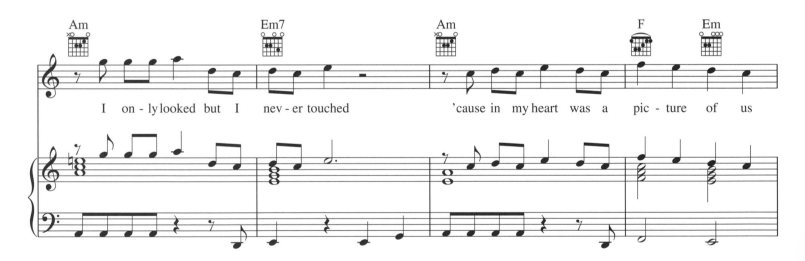

I on - ly looked but I nev - er touched 'cause in my heart was a pic - ture of us

hold - in' hands, __ mak - in' plans and it's luck - y for me __ you un -

yeah. ___ and what you got is what I want. There was a

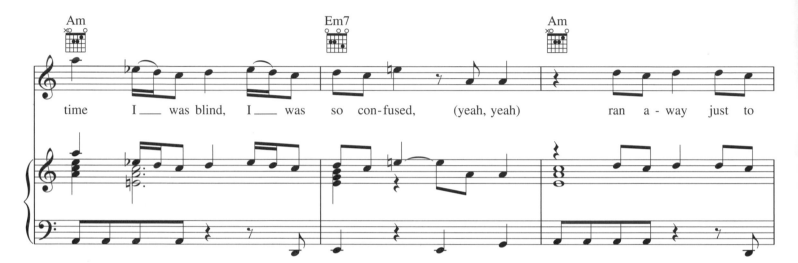

time I ___ was blind, I ___ was so con-fused, (yeah, yeah) ran a - way just to

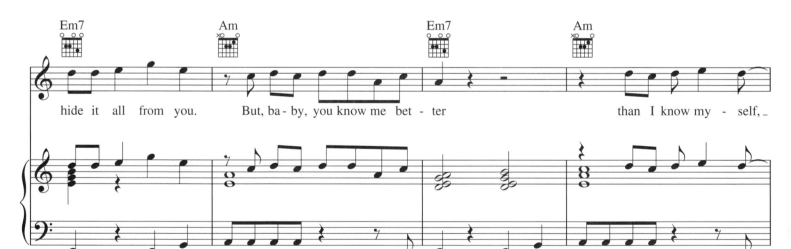

hide it all from you. But, ba - by, you know me bet - ter than I know my - self, __

___ la ooh. ___ They say if you love some-thing let it go. If it comes back, it's yours,

that's how you know it's for keeps, _ yeah, it's ____ for sure. And you're read-y and will-in' to give

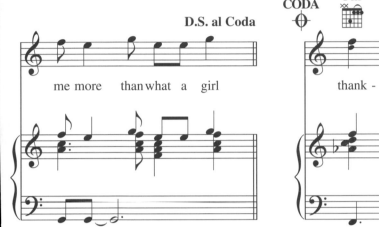

D.S. al Coda

me more than what a girl

CODA Fm   B♭7

thank-ing you ___ for giv-in' it to ____ me, ___

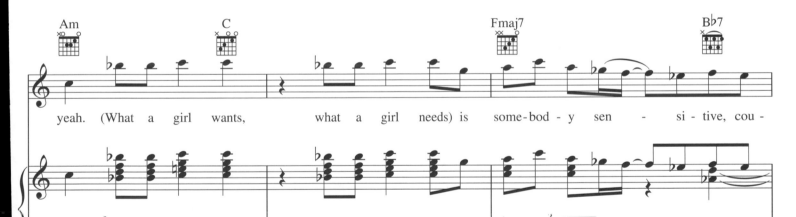

Am   C   Fmaj7   B♭7

yeah. (What a girl wants, what a girl needs) is some-bod-y sen - si - tive, cou-

Am   C

ra-geous, and se-cure ___ like you. ___ (What a girl wants, what a girl needs,) some-

what a girl wants, what a girl needs, what-ev-er keeps me in
What a girl wants,

your arms and I'm thank-ing you for giv-in' it. What a girl

wants, what a girl needs, what-ev-er makes me hap-py sets

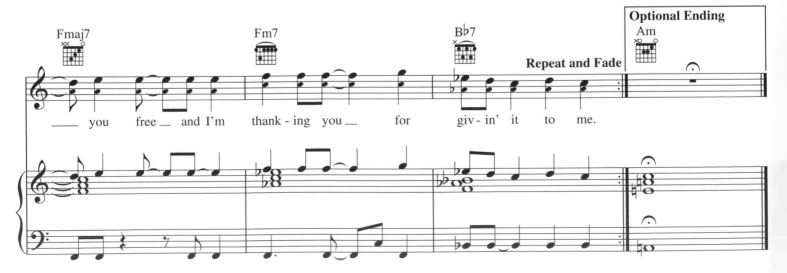

you free and I'm thank-ing you for giv-in' it to me.

Repeat and Fade

Optional Ending

I TURN TO YOU

Words and Music by
DIANE WARREN

*Recorded a half step lower.

© 1996 REALSONGS and WB MUSIC CORP.
All Rights Reserved   Used by Permission

for a love _ to keep _ me safe _ and _ warm, _ I turn to you. _ For the strength _

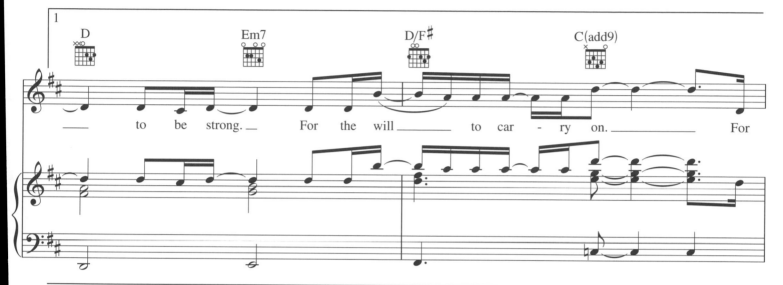

to be strong. _ For the will _____ to car - ry on. _____ For

ev - 'ry - thing _ you do, _____ for ev - 'ry - thing _ that's true, _ I turn _ to you, _

_____ yeah. _ When I lose _

the will __ to win __ __ to be strong. __ For the will __

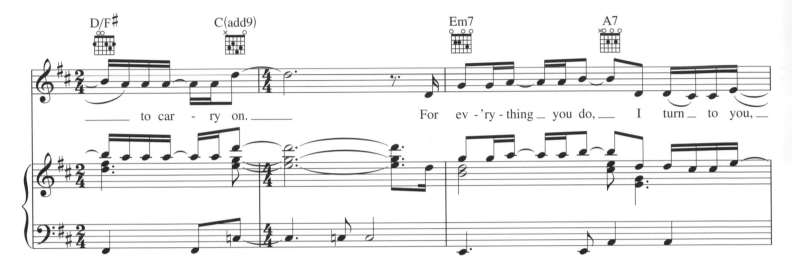

__ to car - ry on. __ For ev -'ry - thing __ you do, __ I turn __ to you, __

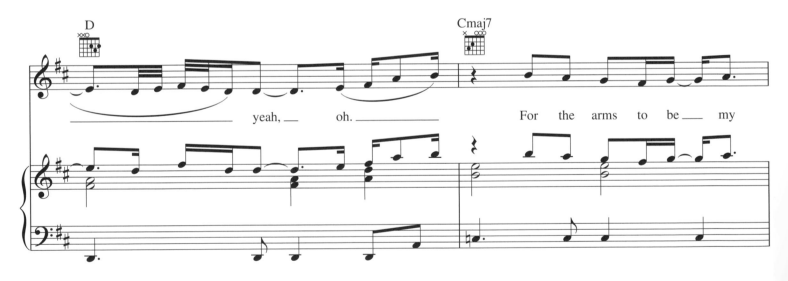

yeah, __ oh. __ For the arms to be __ my

shel - ter through all the rain. __ For truth that will nev - er change. __ For

some-one to lean on. For a heart I can __ re - ly on through an - y - thing. _____ For the __

one who _____ I can __ run _____ to, _____ oh _____

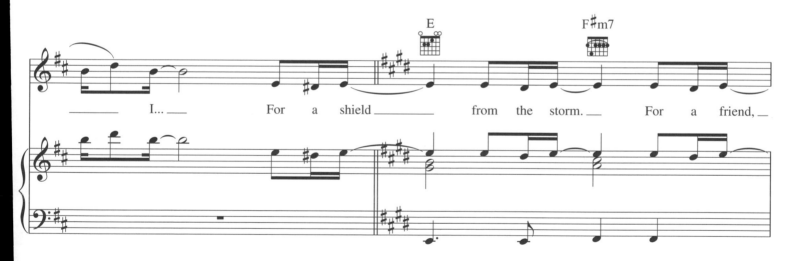

__ I... __ For a shield _____ from the storm. __ For a friend, __

__ for a love __ to keep __ me safe __ and warm, _____ I

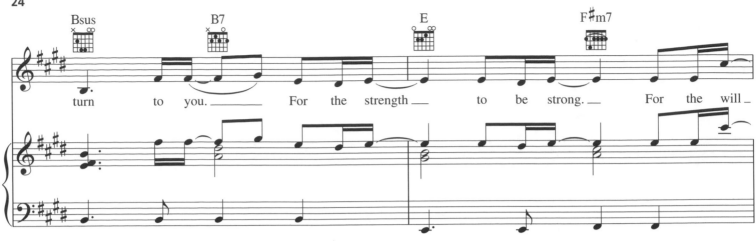

turn to you. _____ For the strength _____ to be strong. _____ For the will _

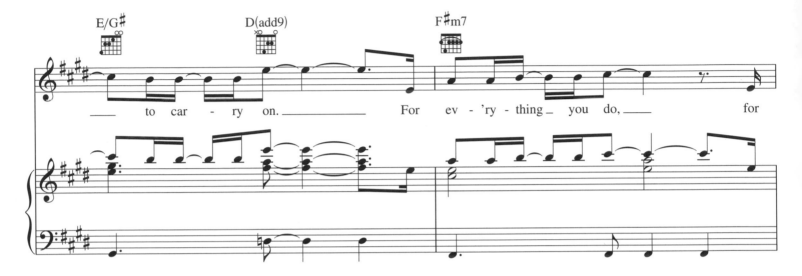

_____ to car - ry on. _____ For ev - 'ry - thing _ you do, _____ for

ev - 'ry - thing _ that's true. _____ For ev - 'ry - thing _ you do, _____ for

ev - 'ry - thing _ that's true _____ I turn _ to you. _____

COME ON OVER BABY
(All I Want Is You)

Words and Music by JOHAN ABERG,
RONALD FAIR, CHRISTINA AGUILERA, ERIC DAWKINS,
GUY ROCHE, PAULI REINIKAINEN, SHELLY PEIKEN,
CHAKA BLACKMON and RAY CHAM

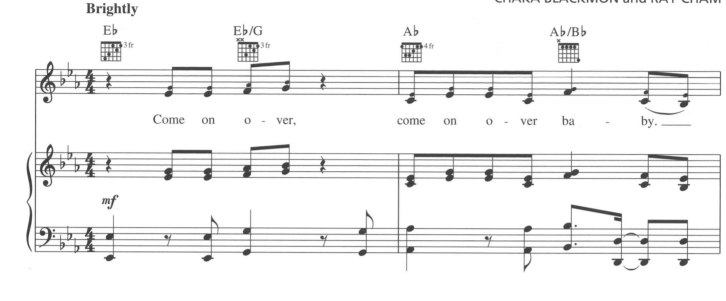

Copyright © 1999, 2000 by Eclectic Music, Universal Music - MGB Songs, Xtina Music, Manuiti L.A., Irving Music, Inc.,
E.D. Duz-It Music, Underdog East Songs, Faircraft Music, Chrysalis Music, Peermusic III, Ltd., Shellayla Songs,
Celebrity Status Entertainment, FSMGI and Vibe Like That Music
All Rights for Eclectic Music in the U.S. and Canada Administered by Universal Music - Careers
All Rights for Xtina Music and Manuiti L.A. Administered by Universal Music - MGB Songs
All Rights for E.D. Duz-It Music and Underdog East Songs Controlled and Administered by Irving Music, Inc.
All Rights for Faircraft Music Controlled and Administered by Universal Music Corp.
All Rights for Shellayla Songs Administered by Peermusic III, Ltd.
All Rights for FSMGI and Vibe Like That Music Administered by State One Songs America
International Copyright Secured   All Rights Reserved

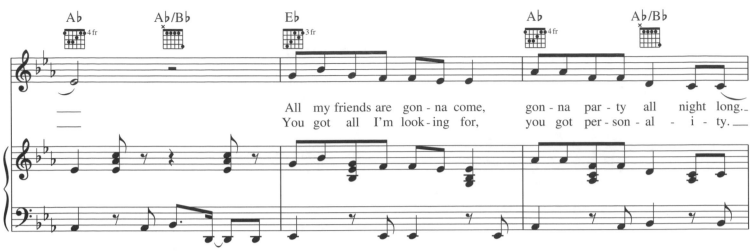

All my friends are gon - na come, gon - na par - ty all night long.
You got all I'm look - ing for, you got per - son - al - i - ty.

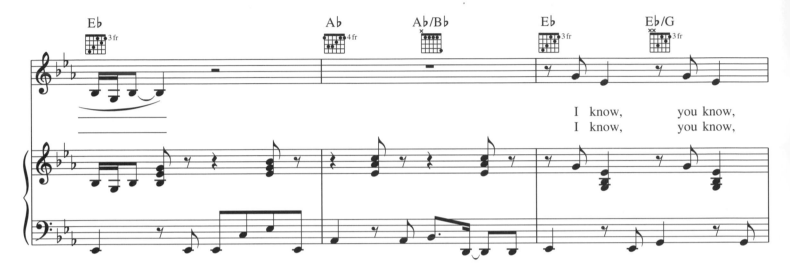

I know, you know,
I know, you know,

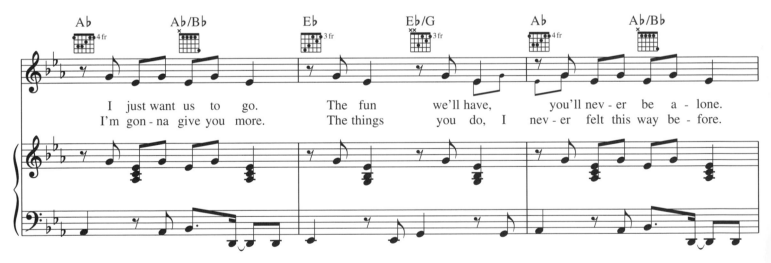

I just want us to go. The fun we'll have, you'll nev - er be a - lone.
I'm gon - na give you more. The things you do, I nev - er felt this way be - fore.

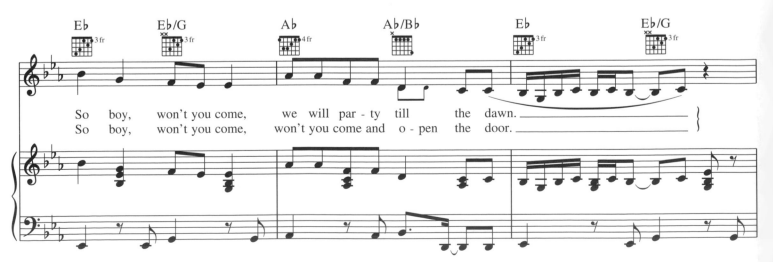

So boy, won't you come, we will par - ty till the dawn.
So boy, won't you come, won't you come and o - pen the door.

Lis - ten to me. _____ (All I want is you.) _____ Come o - ver here ba -

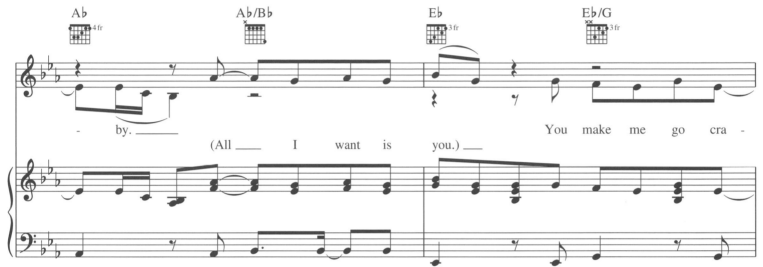

- by. _____ (All _____ I want is you.) _____ You make me go cra -

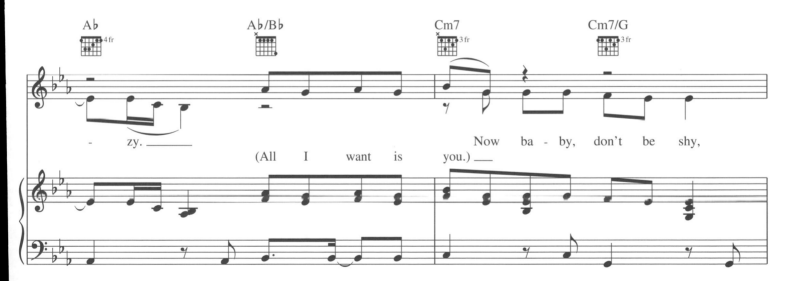

- zy. _____ (All I want is you.) _____ Now ba - by, don't be shy,

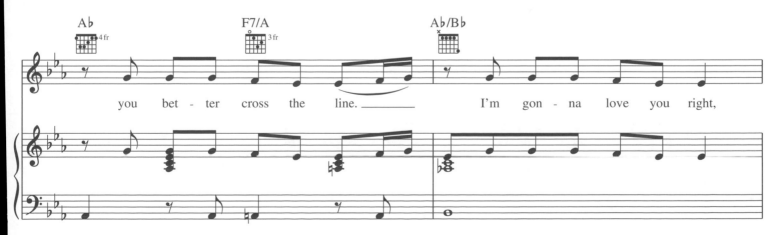

you bet - ter cross the line. _____ I'm gon - na love you right,

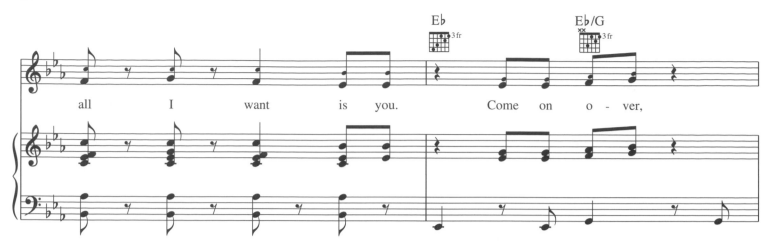

all I want is you. Come on o- ver,

come on o- ver ba - by. Come on o- ver, come on o- ver ba - by.

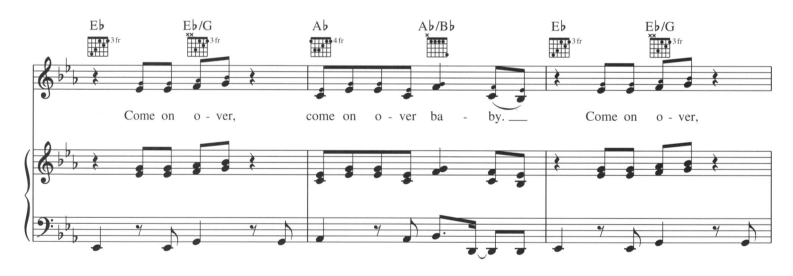

Come on o- ver, come on o- ver ba - by. Come on o- ver,

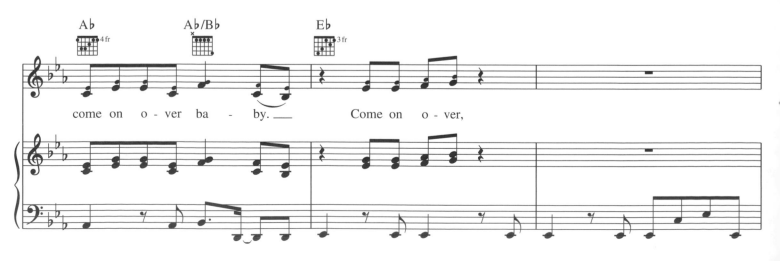

come on o- ver ba - by. Come on o- ver,

you bet - ter cross the line. ____ I'm gon - na love you right, 'cause all I want is you. ____ (All I want is

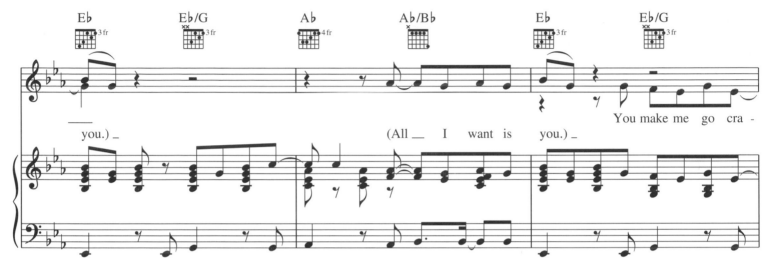

____ you.) __ (All __ I want is you.) __ You make me go cra -

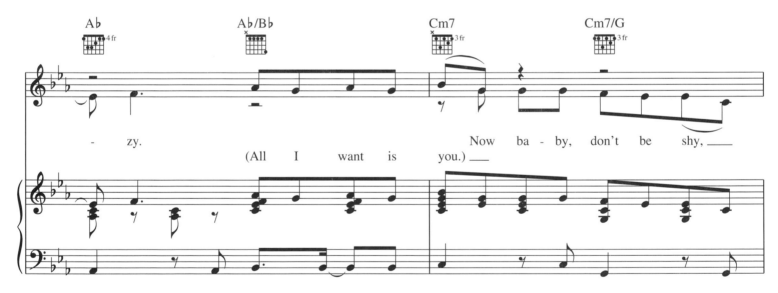

- zy. (All I want is you.) ____ Now ba - by, don't be shy, ____

you bet - ter cross the line. __ I'm gon - na love you right, 'cause all I want is you.

DIRRTY

Words by CHRISTINA AGUILERA
Music by BALEWA MUHAMMAD,
DANA STINSON, REGGIE NOBLE
and JASPER CAMERON

Copyright © 2002 by Universal Music - Careers, Xtina Music, Universal - PolyGram International Tunes, Inc., Jahqae Joints Music, Warner-Tamerlane Publishing Corp.,
Dayna's Day Publishing, WB Music Corp., Funky Noble Productions, Inc. and Ostaf Songs
All Rights for Xtina Music Administered by Universal Music - Careers
All Rights for Jahqae Joints Music Controlled and Administered by Universal - PolyGram International Tunes, Inc.
International Copyright Secured   All Rights Reserved

Ring the a - larm... *and I'm throw - in' el - bows.* *Uhh... let me loose.*

Ooh, I'm o - ver - due; __ gim - me some room, ____ com - in' through. __

Ah, heat is up. __ La - dies fel - las, drop your cups. ____

Paid my dues; I'm in the mood. Me and my girls come to shake the room. __

Bod - ies packed front to back. __ Move your ass, I like that. __

D. J.'s spin - nin', show your hands. __ Let's get dirr - ty, that's my jam. __ I

Tight hip - hug - gers, low for sho'. ____ Shake a lit - tle some - thin' on the flo'. ____ I

G5

It's ex - plo - sive, speak - ers are pump - in'. Still jump - in', six in the morn - in'.
Let's get o - pen, cause a com - mo - tion. Still go - in' eight in the morn - in'.

Ta - ble danc - in', glass - es are crash - in'. No ques - tion, time for some ac - tion.
There's no stop - pin', we keep it pop - pin'. Hard rock - in', ev - 'ry - one's talk - in'.

Tem - per - 'tures up; (Can you feel it?) 'bout to __ e - rupt. Some one get my
Give all __ you got; (Give it to me.) just hit __ the spot. Gon - na get my

N.C.

girls, get your boys, gon-na make some noise. _____ Gon-na get
girls, get your boys, gon-na make some noise. _____

G5

row-dy. Gon-na get a lit-tle un-ru-ly. Get it fired up in a

hur-ry. Wan-na get dirr-ty. It's a-bout time that I came to start the

par-ty. Sweat drip-pin' off o' my bod-y. Danc-in' get-tin' just a lit-tle

when we take it to the park - ing lot, ___ and I bet you, some - bod - y's gon - na call the cops. ___ Uh -

oh, (Uh - oh,) here we go. (here we go.) Oh, _____

_____ yeah, ___ yeah. Rap: *(See additional lyrics)*

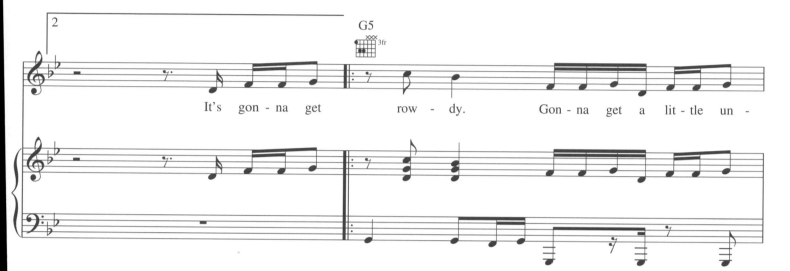

It's gon - na get row - dy. Gon - na get a lit - tle un -

- ru - ly. Get it fired up in a hur - ry. Wan - na get dirr - ty.

It's a - bout time that I came to start the par - ty. Sweat drip - pin' off o' my

bod - y.   Danc - in' get - tin' just a lit - tle naugh - ty.   Wan - na get dirr - ty.

It's a - bout time for my ar - ri - val.   It's a - bout time for my ar - ri - val.   *Uhh, what?*

Additional Lyrics

Rap: Hot damn! Got the jam, like a summer show.
I keep my pawn lookin' like a crash dummy drove.
My gear look like the bait got my money froze.
But there are presidents I pimp like Teddy Ro'.
Got the one that excites ya deepest,
At the media shine, I'm shinin' with both of the sleeves up.
Yo Christina, what happened here?
My black, live and in color, like Rodman hair.

The club is packed, the bar is filled, they're waitin' for
Sister to act like Lauren Hill. Frankly,
It's so black, no bargain deals, I'll drop a
Four-wheel drive with foreign wheels. Throw it up!
Bet you this is Brick City, you heard o' that.
We're blessed and hung low, like Bernie Mack.
Dogs, let 'em out; women, let 'em in.
It's like I'm O.D.B., that what they're thinkin'.

FIGHTER

Words and Music by CHRISTINA AGUILERA
and SCOTT STORCH

(Spoken:) After all you put me through,   *you'd think I'd despise you.*   *But in the end, I wanna thank you, 'cause you*

made me that much stronger.   Well, I   thought I knew you, think-ing   that you were true. Guess I,

saw it com - ing, all of   your back-stab - bing, just so

I could - n't trust; called your bluff, time is up, 'cause I've had _ e - nough. _ You were

you could cash in   on a   good thing be - fore I'd re - al - ize _ your game. _ I heard

Copyright © 2002 by Universal Music - Careers, Xtina Music, Scott Storch Music and TVT Music Inc.
All Rights for Xtina Music Administered by Universal Music - Careers
International Copyright Secured All Rights Reserved

Made me learn a lit-tle bit fast - er, __ made __ my skin a lit-tle bit thick - er, __

makes me __ that much smart - er; _____ so thanks for mak - ing me a fight - er. __

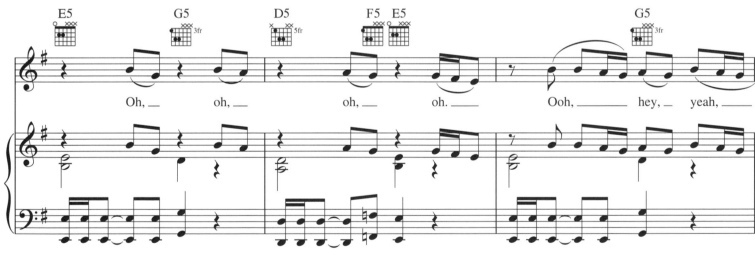

Oh, __ oh, __ oh, __ oh. __ Ooh, __ hey, __ yeah, __

__ oh. Nev -er thanks for mak - ing me a fight - er. __

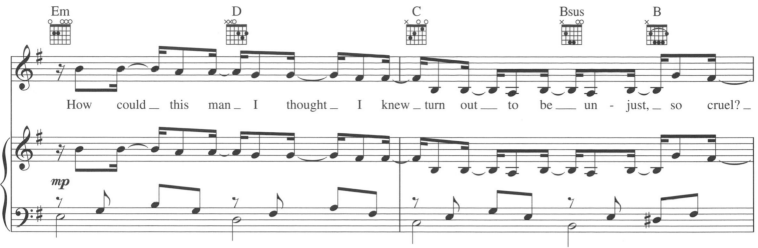

How could _ this man _ I thought _ I knew _ turn out _ to be _ un - just, _ so cruel? _

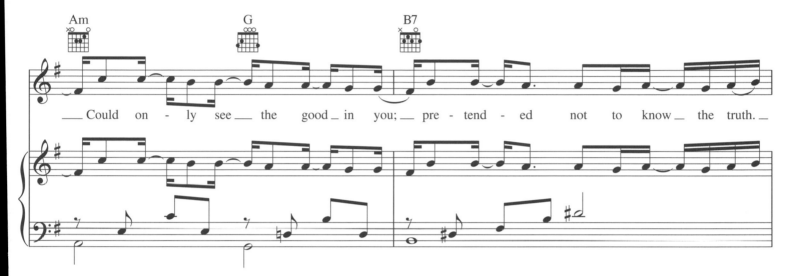

_ Could on - ly see _ the good _ in you; _ pre - tend - ed not to know _ the truth. _

You tried _ to hide _ your lies, _ dis - guise _ your - self _ through liv - ing in _ de - nial, _

_ but in _ the end _ you'll see: _____ You won't stop me!

44

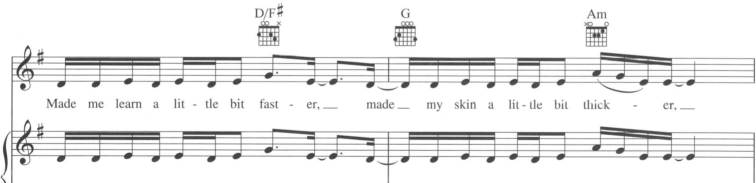

BEAUTIFUL

Words and Music by
LINDA PERRY

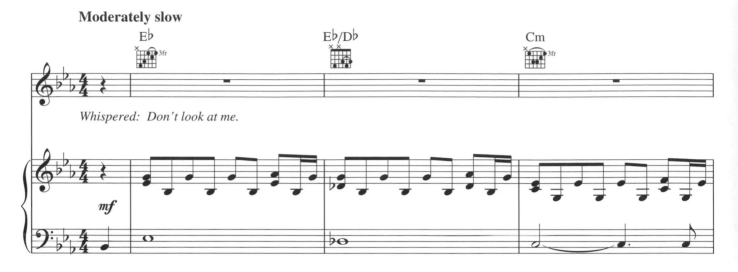

Whispered: Don't look at me.

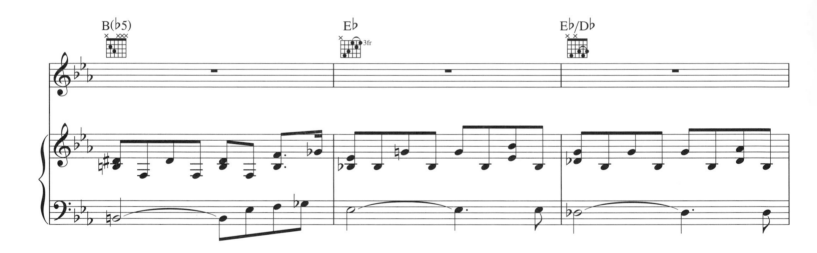

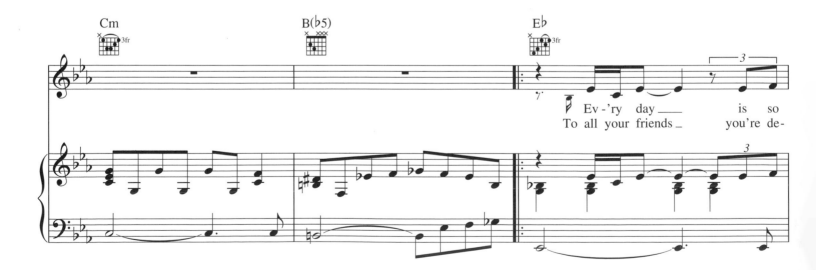

Ev-'ry day ___ is so
To all your friends ___ you're de-

Copyright © 2002 Sony/ATV Music Publishing LLC and Stuck In The Throat Music
All Rights Administered by Sony/ATV Music Publishing LLC, 8 Music Square West, Nashville, TN 37203
International Copyright Secured   All Rights Reserved

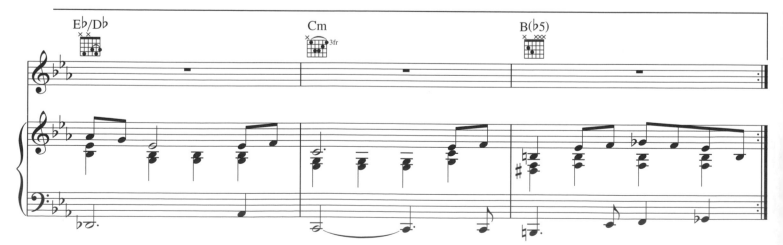

So don't you __ bring me down to-day. _____ No mat - ter what __ we do. __

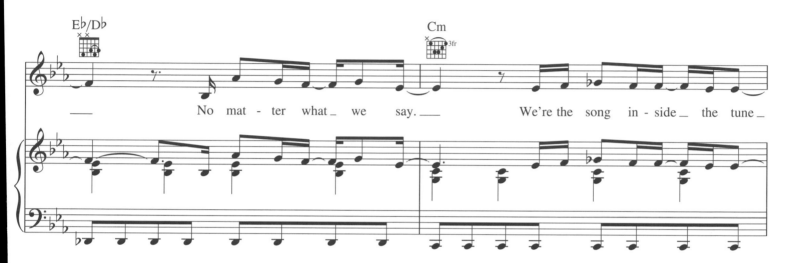

__ No mat - ter what __ we say. __ We're the song in - side __ the tune __

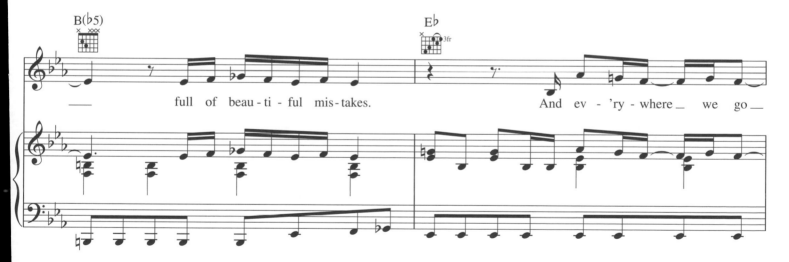

__ full of beau - ti - ful mis - takes. And ev - 'ry - where __ we go __

__ the sun will al - ways shine. __ And to - mor - row we might a - wake __

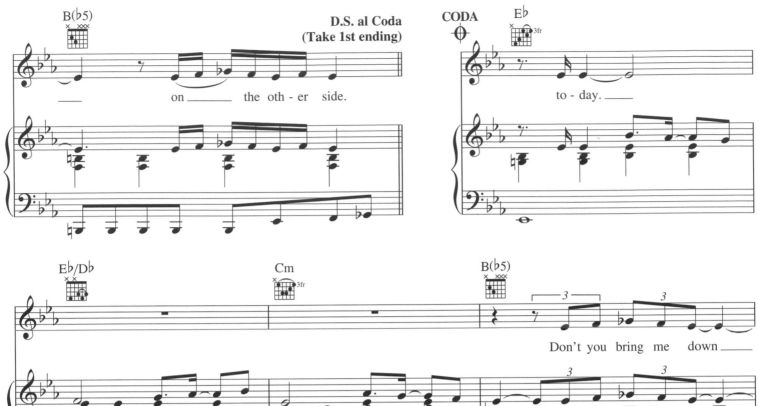

on ___ the oth-er side.

D.S. al Coda
(Take 1st ending)

CODA

to - day. ___

Don't you bring me down ___

to - day, ___ yeah, _____ ooh. ___

Don't you bring me down ___ um ___ to - day.

AIN'T NO OTHER MAN

Words and Music by CHRISTINA AGUILERA,
KARA DioGUARDI, CHRIS MARTIN,
CHARLES ROANE and HAROLD BEATTY

Copyright © 2006 by Universal Music - Careers, Xtina Music, Bug Music Inc., Gifted Pearl Music, Works Of Mart, Inc., Tricia Sounds Music and Iza Music Corp.
All Rights for Xtina Music Administered by Universal Music - Careers
All Rights for Iza Music Corp. Administered by The Clyde Otis Music Group, Inc.
International Copyright Secured   All Rights Reserved

I don't know what you did boy, but, you had it

and I've been hooked ev - er since. _____ Told my

moth - er, my broth - er, my sis - ter and my friends. Told the oth - ers, my lov - ers, both

past and pres - ent tense that ev - 'ry time I see you ev - 'ry - thing starts mak - in' sense. _____

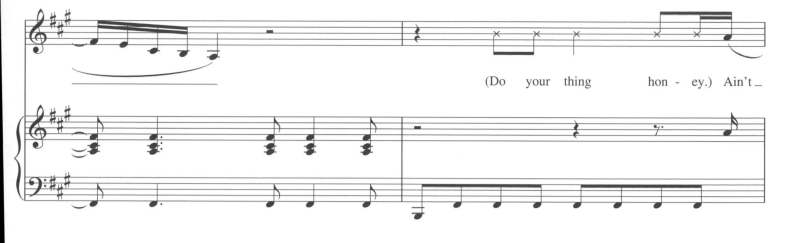

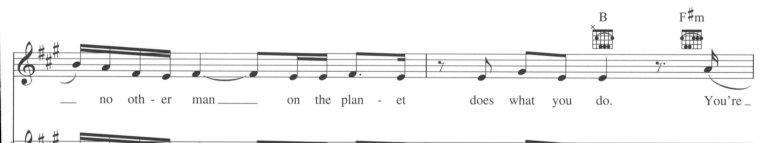

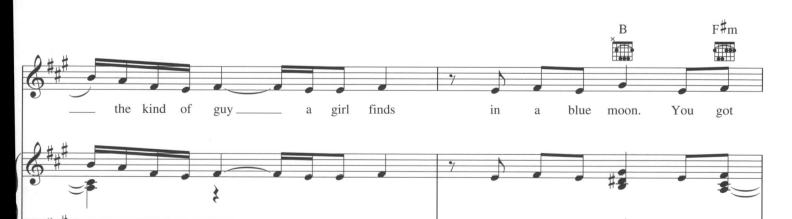

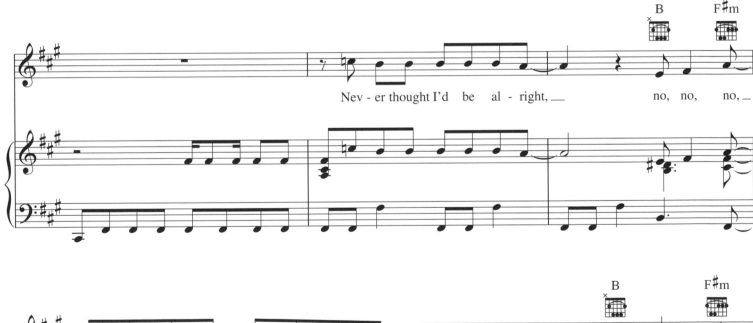

What was cloud-y now is clear, ____ yeah, yeah. __ You're the light that I need-ed. __

_____ You got what I want, boy, and I want

it, so keep on giv-in' it up. _____ Tell your

moth-er, your broth-er, your sis-ter and your friends. Tell the oth-ers, your lov-ers bet-ter

You're the on - ly one who's ev - er passed ev - 'ry test.

Ain't __ no oth - er man __ that can stand

up next to you. Ain't __ no oth - er man __ on the plan - et

does what you do. You're __ the kind of guy __ a girl finds

CANDYMAN

Words and Music by CHRISTINA AGUILERA
and LINDA PERRY

Copyright © 2006 by Universal Music - Careers, Xtina Music, Sony/ATV Music Publishing LLC and Stuck In The Throat Music
All Rights for Xtina Music Administered by Universal Music - Careers
All Rights for Sony/ATV Music Publishing LLC and Stuck In The Throat Music Administered by Sony/ATV Music Publishing LLC, 8 Music Square West, Nashville, TN 37203
International Copyright Secured   All Rights Reserved

Hey, hey, _____ yeah, _____ uh. I

met him out for din - ner on a Fri - day night; _____ he
took me to the Spi - der Club at Hol - ly - wood and Vine; _____ we

real - ly had me work - in' up an ap - pe - tite. _____ He
drank _____ cham - pagne _____ and we danced all night. _____ We

A7

had tat - toos _____ up and down his arm. _____ There's
shook the pa - pa - raz - zi for a big sur - prise; _____ the

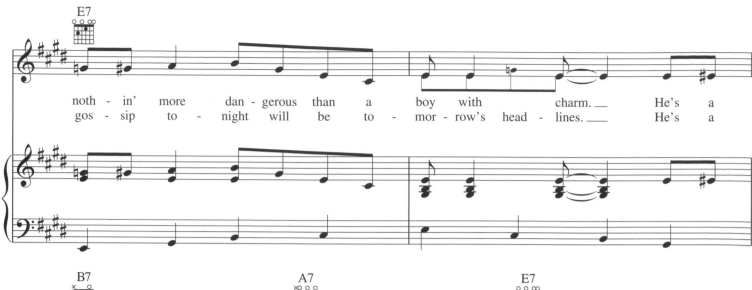

noth - in' more dan - ger - ous than a boy with charm. __ He's a
gos - sip to - night will be to - mor - row's head - lines. __ He's a

one - stop shop, __ makes the pan - ties drop. __
one - stop shop, __ makes my cher - ry pop. __ He's a sweet - talk - in' sug - ar - coat - ed

can - dy - man, __ a sweet - talk - in' sug - ar - coat - ed can - dy - man. __

Ooh yeah, _____ yeah. _____

Sha - doo - bah dee - bah doo - bah dwee - bop bow.___ He's a one - stop shop,___ makes my

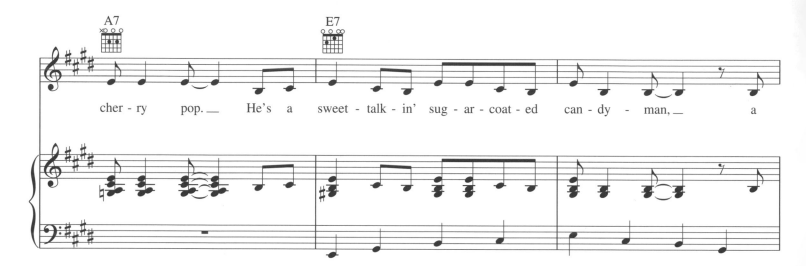

cher - ry pop.___ He's a sweet - talk - in' sug - ar - coat - ed can - dy - man,___ a

sweet - talk - in' sug - ar - coat - ed can - dy - man.___

Oh whoa,_____ yeah,_____ ee,_____ yeah.___

can - dy - man.) _ *Male:* sip - pin' from a bot - tle of vod - ka dou - ble wine.

Female: (Can - dy - man, _ can - dy - man, _ sweet, sug - ar,

can - dy - man.) _ He's a one - stop, got - cha hot, mak - in' all the pan - ties drop,

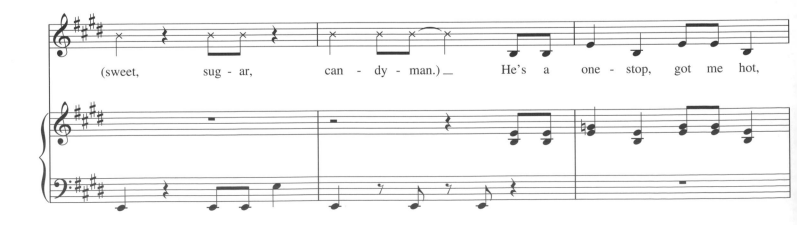

(sweet, sug - ar, can - dy - man.) _ He's a one - stop, got me hot,

real big ah! ___ He's a sweet - talk - in' sug - ar - coat - ed can - dy - man, ___ a

sweet - talk - in' sug - ar - coat - ed can - dy - man, ___ a sweet - talk - in' sug - ar - coat - ed

can - dy - man, ___ a sweet - talk - in' sug - ar - coat - ed can - dy - man. ___

(Can - dy - man.) ___

(Can - dy - man.) _ (Can - dy - man.) _ (Can - dy - man, _

N.C.

can - dy - man, _ can - dy - man, _ can - dy - man.) _

Male: Tar - zan and Jane were swing - in' on a vine, (Tar - zan and Jane were swing -

- in' on a vine,) sip - pin' from a bot - tle of vod -

HURT

Words and Music by CHRISTINA AGUILERA,
LINDA PERRY and MARK RONSON

Copyright © 2006 by Universal Music - Careers, Xtina Music, Sony/ATV Music Publishing LLC, Stuck In The Throat Music, EMI Music Publishing Ltd. and Inouye Music
All Rights for Xtina Music Administered by Universal Music - Careers
All Rights for Sony/ATV Music Publishing LLC and Stuck In The Throat Music Administered by Sony/ATV Music Publishing LLC, 8 Music Square West, Nashville, TN 37203
All Rights for EMI Music Publishing Ltd. in the United States and Canada Controlled and Administered by EMI Blackwood Music Inc.
International Copyright Secured   All Rights Reserved

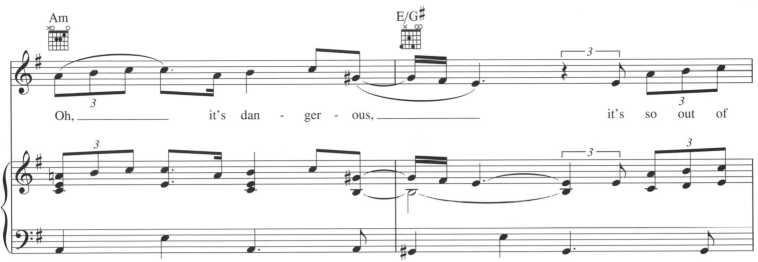

Oh, _____ it's dan - ger - ous, _____ it's so out of

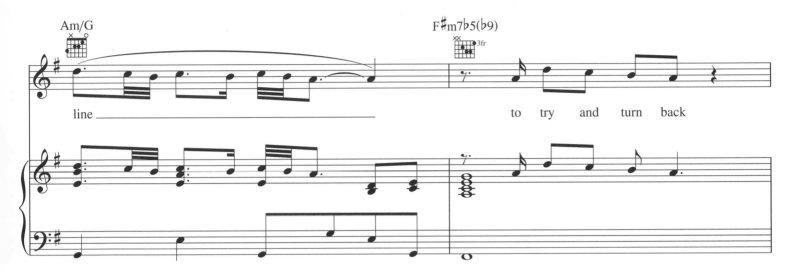

line _____ to try and turn back

time. _____

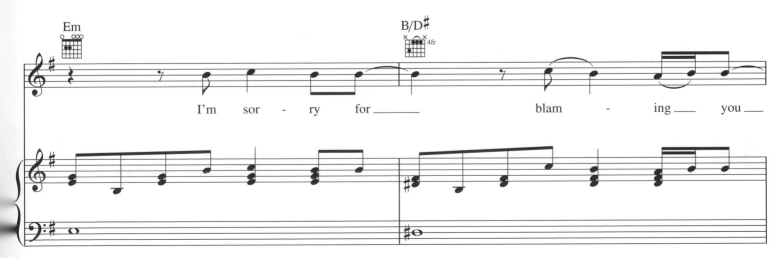

I'm sor - ry for _____ blam - ing _____ you _____

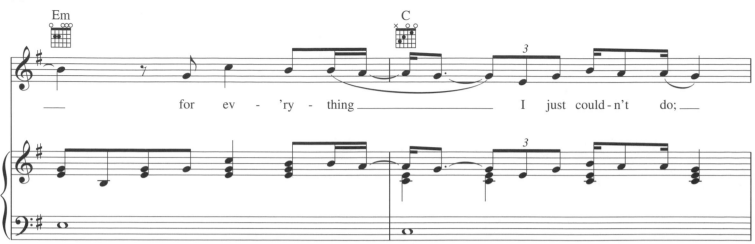

for ev - 'ry - thing _____ I just could - n't do; ___

and I've hurt ____ my - self... _____

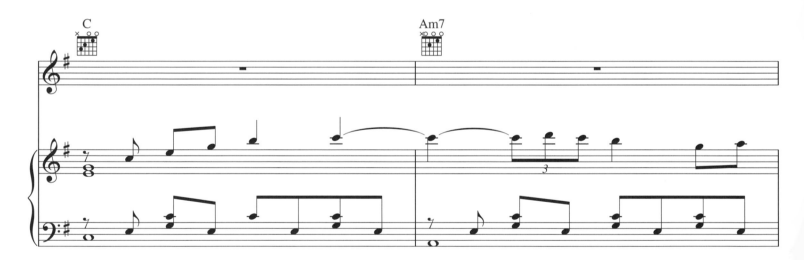

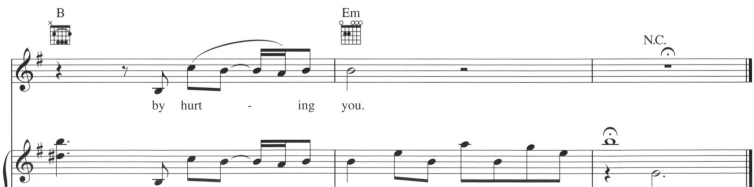

by hurt - ing you.

KEEPS GETTIN' BETTER

Words and Music by CHRISTINA AGUILERA
and LINDA PERRY

Driving Shuffle

Step back, gon-na come at you fast,__ I'm driv-ing out of con-trol__ and get-ting

Kiss, kiss, gon-na tell you right now,__ I'll make it sweet on the lips__ as it can

Copyright © 2008 by Universal Music - Careers, Xtina Music, Sony/ATV Music Publishing LLC and Stuck In The Throat Music
All Rights for Xtina Music Administered by Universal Music - Careers
All Rights for Sony/ATV Music Publishing LLC and Stuck In The Throat Music Administered by Sony/ATV Music Publishing LLC, 8 Music Square West, Nashville, TN 37203
International Copyright Secured   All Rights Reserved

read - y to crash. _ Won't stop shak - ing up what I can. _ I serve it
knock you _ out. _ Shut up, I don't care what you say. _ 'Cause when we're

Bb5

up in a shot, _ so suck it down like a man. _ So, ba - by, yes, I
both in the ring, _ you're gon - na like it my way. _ Yeah, ba - by, there's a

Ab   Gm7

know what I am, _ and, no, I don't give a damn, _ and you'll be lov - ing it. _
vil - lain in me, _ so sex - y, sour _ and sweet, _ and you'll be lov - ing it. _

Fm   Ab   Gm7   C7

Some days I'm a su - per bitch _ up to my old tricks, _ but it won't last for - ev - er.

Next day I'm your su-per girl, __ out to save the world, __ and it keeps get-ting bet-ter.

Hold _____ on, _____ it keeps get-ting bet-ter.

Hold _____ on, _____ it keeps get-ting bet-ter. In the

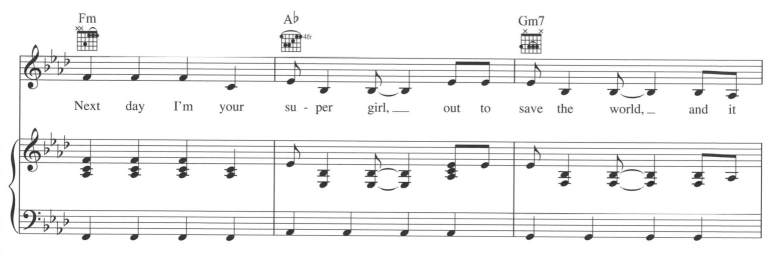

Next day I'm your su - per girl, ___ out to save the world, ___ and it

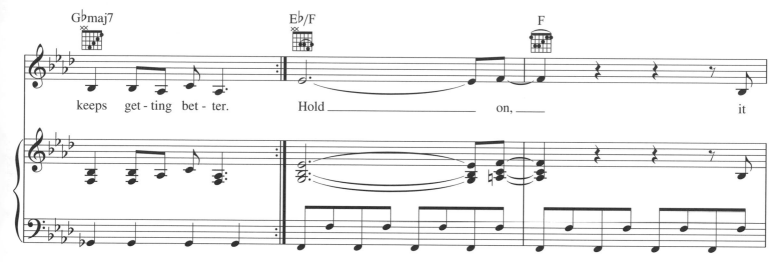

keeps get - ting bet - ter. Hold _____ on, ___ it

keeps get - ting bet - ter. Hold _____ on, _

___ it keeps get - ting bet - ter.

DYNAMITE

Words and Music by CHRISTINA AGUILERA
and LINDA PERRY

Moderate Techno beat

Copyright © 2008 by Universal Music - Careers, Xtina Music, Sony/ATV Music Publishing LLC and Stuck In The Throat Music
All Rights for Xtina Music Administered by Universal Music - Careers
All Rights for Sony/ATV Music Publishing LLC and Stuck In The Throat Music Administered by Sony/ATV Music Publishing LLC, 8 Music Square West, Nashville, TN 37203
International Copyright Secured   All Rights Reserved

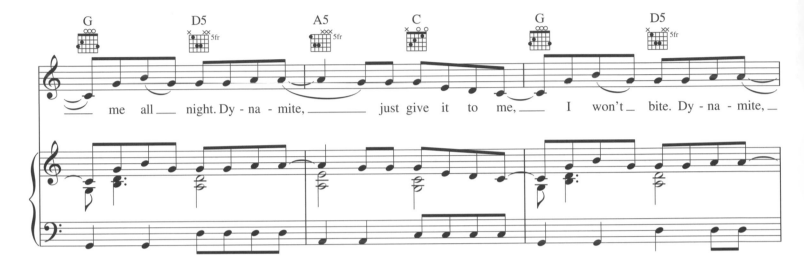

Caught up in this mo-ment I was

hyp - no - tized. __ Shake this feel - in', got me par - a - lyzed. __ I

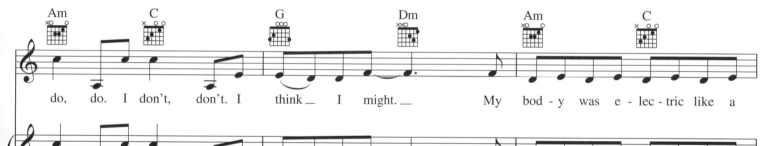

do, do. I don't, don't. I think __ I might. __ My bod - y was e - lec - tric like a

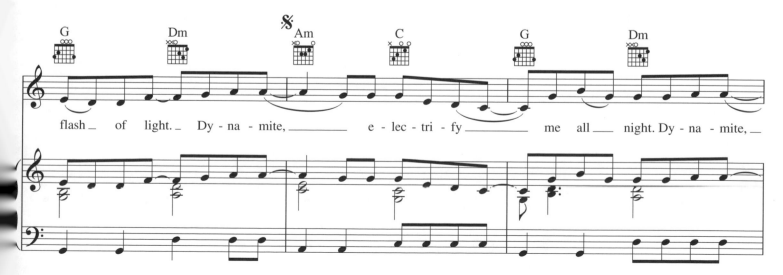

flash __ of light. __ Dy - na - mite, _____ e - lec - tri - fy _____ me all __ night. Dy - na - mite, __

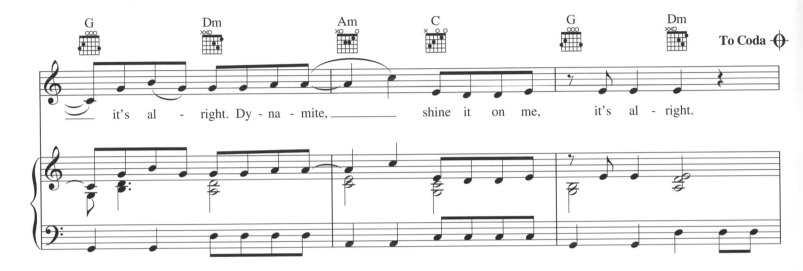

Uh oh, _____ uh oh, _____ uh, oh, ___ oh, ___ oh. ___ Danc-in' 'til the morn-in' on a

vel - vet sky. ___ Danc-in' 'til the morn-in' on a vel - vet sky. ___

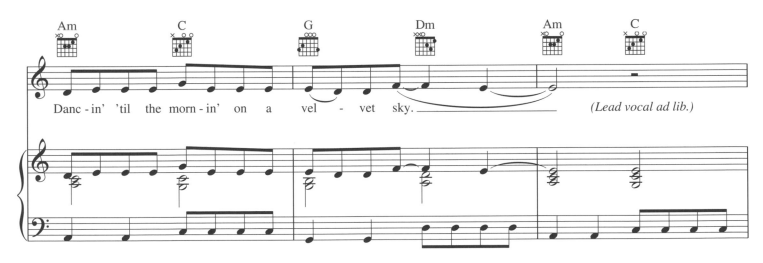

Danc-in' 'til the morn-in' on a vel - vet sky. _____ (Lead vocal ad lib.)

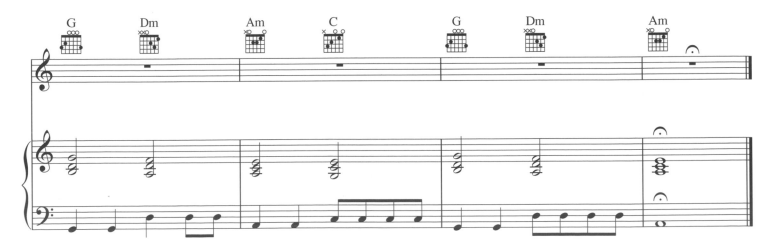